EveryBody EATS

Get Cooking, Get Healthy, Get Happy

ALISSA MONTELEONE CHHC, AADP

The information included in this book is for educational purposes only. It is not intended nor implied to be a substitute for professional medical advice. The reader should always consult his or her healthcare provider to determine the appropriate information for their own situation and if they have any questions regarding a medical condition or treatment plan.

Book Design by Alissa Monteleone
Food Photography by Alissa Monteleone

"As a trained personal chef, I love good food. As a certified health coach I know how good food nourishes our bodies. As a working mom, I know how important having energy and being healthy is for me, my family and my business. I feel the best I have in almost 30 years. I appreciate this opportunity to share with you some of the lessons of my journey and I encourage you to use this book to continue your own journey toward the health and happiness you deserve. Simply apply good thinking to the choices you make each day and you will reap the benefits."

Alissa is a certified a Holistic Health Coach by the American Association of Drugless Practitioners and a certified personal chef by the United States Personal Chef Association. She is also certified by the American Council on Exercise as a Weight Management and Lifestyle Coach. She earned a BA from the University of Connecticut and holds a masters certificate in Critcal and Creative Thinking from The University of Massachusetts. She is a graduate of the Institute of Integrative Nutrition and has earned continuing Education Units from Purchase College, State University of New York.

To my family:

MOO thank you.

TDAX forever.

Mom and Dad for everything.

SCA's rule.

EveryBody Eats

About this book

*"Everybody eats because Every Body needs to eat. We
must honor our body's need for nutrition while being
mindful of the role food plays in everybody's life."*

EveryBody Eats is about **YOU**. It's about you needing food every day and how you can meet that need in a healthy way. We, as humans, are designed to eat for 2 reasons, survival and pleasure; it is the priority of these reasons that has become an issue for many of us. Eating is meant to bring us pleasure. The enjoyment of the aromas, the flavors, the pleasing textures combined with the community that comes together around food is all part of our biology. It helps ensure that we will eat since we need to eat to survive.

Enter the need. Our bodies need food; more importantly we need the nutrients and energy that food provides us. If we don't eat, we don't flourish. If the food we eat lacks in either nutrients (vitamins, minerals, enzymes, etc.) or in energy (calories) we may survive but we again, do not flourish.

EveryBody Eats is also about feeding the people you care about. Kids, friends, family, they all eat; and when they come together, it can become stressful. They may not want to or be able to eat the same thing. He hates broccoli, she can't have wheat and that's WAY too spicy for him. Arrggg! So, I came up with some clever (well I think they are clever) tricks to overcome stress when it comes to meal time.

EveryBody Eats is not a diet. I do not profess to know what you should eat for your optimal health. I do not provide you with the 5 best foods to cure anything. Why? Mainly because I don't know and I am not convinced anyone knows. The medical community comes out with diametrically opposed theories of what we should be eating every 2-5 years. The booming diet industry rolls out a new "ultimate" plan at least every 6 months. It drives me crazy!

Of course, I used to fall for these "get thin quick" gimmicks. Each time feeling more determined to have the will power to stick to the program. Each time I would invest in whatever supplements, powders, new food and mental attitude they prescribe and each time I would fail. Inevitably my health and happiness suffered and I would eat to make myself feel better. I spent plenty of time falling prey to poor body image, fad diets and abusive coping mechanisms that began to take their toll on more than my appearance.

> *Being overweight is one thing, being addicted to food both emotionally and physically complicates matters. Throw in some alcohol and bad decisions are right around the corner. When I look back, 2 things strike me: one, I seemed to know what I was doing and yet continued to do it and two, every time I tried to get out, it seemed more comfortable to stay trapped and continue in the downward spiral.*

> *Wow, I can hardly believe that I am talking about me. I consider myself smart, confident and fortunate and yet, I treated myself and my body with such disdain and disrespect, I can barely write it down. So why am I?*

> *I believe life is awesome; I was just less convinced that I was awesome. Most people that know me may laugh at that statement since I always talk a good talk of positive self worth. Sadly, my over confident outward voice spoke very loudly in an effort to drown out my self doubting, inner voice. To this day, I doubt you could find a handful of people that would say I ever lacked confidence. In fact, I even had myself convinced until I realized that I was out of control and it was starting to hurt people other than myself.*

Finally, after having my first child at 36 years old, I realized I needed to hold myself accountable for my wellbeing.   I started taking responsibility for my health and started listening to my own body. I learned to cook real food using simple methods and recipes. I stopped buying foods that I knew I used as an emotional crutch. I began to notice how I felt after eating different foods and began to cut down, and sometimes eliminate, anything that made me feel less than good. It took time and often it was two steps forward and one step back.

I continue to refine and adjust what I eat as I learn more and as life places different demands on my body.   I strive to nourish my body and not to solve my momentary discomforts with food. I also allow myself to indulge every once in a while and just enjoy it. Now food serves me and no longer controls me.

That's why I wrote this book and why its main goal is to support and encourage you to take back your own health and happiness.

Over the years I have learned a lot about nutrition. I read the studies and listen to the experts share their latest findings. Based on all the information I have gathered thus far, I believe we have a good grasp on how parts of the body work independently; however, we have a way to go before we understand how the body brings it all together.

It is fascinating how the body processes and uses food. Individuals survive and thrive in so many diverse circumstances. Indigenous people can survive off animal protein even though don't have daily access to fresh fruits and veggies and yet people live in places where they eat a plant based diet and consume little to no animal protein. How is this possible? Is it their blood type or their genetic code? Is the quality of one groups' health superior to the other? You can find a research defending both.

For me, it comes down to this, I am not a scientist; I am a human being trying to figure it out as I go. I take in information, I think about it, I experiment and I create practical approaches based on what make sense. In EveryBody Eats, I share with you ideas on meal preparation and presentation aimed to maximize your time and minimize your stress so you can provide healthy meals that just about everybody will enjoy.

There is a ton of information, research and theories out there. Recipes, cooking shows and health blogs abound. You want to know how to peel an apple with power tools, there is a video (truly – it is actually very cool). There will always be more and more to learn and try. There will always be the next best thing no matter what you do or when you do it – so I say just start someplace and go from there.

My intention for this book is to encourage you to start by cooking real food using simple recipes and then keep going.   If you hate every recipe in this book, cross them out and redo it all; as long as you have invested in the process, you and I have both succeeded.

A NOTE ABOUT THE FOOD AND FOOD PHOTOGRAPHY

Everything in this book is real.   I created these recipes over time in my kitchen for my family and myself. I did not develop them in a test kitchen for the sake of writing a book. There were no assistants to help get things ready, make things look pretty or clean the kitchen when I was done. My prep cook is not yet 4 years old and my taste testers have my unconditional love so they tell me like it is for better or for worse.. You may notice I use the same dishes and backgrounds for most the pictures. That is because I took the pictures and then served the food.

When I decided to write this book, I did research food photography. It is fascinating. Professionals take hours to get a photo shoot put together for just a few recipes. Things get spritzed, tucked and fluffed; they even use spray paint. Then the lighting and lenses and the equipment…it is crazy. Needless to say, I did not do that. I used a camera with a flash in my kitchen. What you see is what we ate.

I did attempt to make the pictures look nice. I experimented with angles and played with the zoom. I had fun and I hope you will have fun too. Whenever you come up with a keeper recipe, write it down, take a picture, print it and pop it in the book. It's really cool to have a book of all your favorite recipes so take advantage of the chance to do it right here!

Where to Start

"Start by doing something that you know must
be better then what you are doing now...."

Over the past 30 years of dealing with eating issues, I finally figured out the best place to start is wherever you are now. Start doing something. Start doing something that you know must be better then what you are doing now and then...here's the catch...be willing to let go of the parts of the approach that don't work for you and move on to the next approach. Play around with that approach, take what works, ditch what doesn't and move on again. I believe the fancy name for this is trial and error.

The little voice in your head may be saying, "Really? Really?! I have been down this path so many times...I have trialed and errored myself silly!"

GREAT! That means you are that much farther ahead in your own process. You have lots of research and experience to draw upon.

Hear me out. The reason programs and plans don't work for you is because they belong to someone else. **THEY** figured out what worked for **THEM** and now they want **YOU** to do it too and achieve the same results. This approach has two issues. One, they are sharing with you the streamlined, nicely packaged, step-by-step process that they figured out AFTER they actually achieved the results. The blood, sweat, cheating and swearing has been edited out. Two, even if I am mistaken about number 1 and they are sharing with you the raw, straight up facts of their daily process, it is still THEIR process. They figured out what worked for them based on their body type, preferences, schedule, daily struggles, past demons etc. Unless you are their clone and are able to shadow them in everyday life...chances are you will need to make adaptations in order for it to work for you.

Okay, so now what?

Now you look within and decide; are you willing to take charge of your health? Are you willing to take responsibility for your actions and thoughts? Are you willing to accept where you are and have some fun figuring this thing out for yourself?

If you are willing to own this process, you will know how to get healthy for the rest of your life.

So…

Are you willing to take charge of your health?

Answer here:

How to Choose Where to Start

Over the diets (yes, I can measure my life in diets as much as years) I have found commonalities that make sense for me. Again, I say "for me" for a reason. I believe in a concept put forth by Joshua Rosenthal, founder of the Institute of Integrative Nutrition called *Bio Individuality*. Essentially, when it comes to the best food choices, one size does not fit all. Each person's nutritional and situational needs vary. Plus, what works today may not work tomorrow even for the same person.

For example, when you are a child you need different nutritional support than you do as an adult. If as an adult you decided to become more physically active, you will need to adjust your food accordingly. If you start to travel a lot, you will need to adjust again based on the physiological demands traveling puts on your body.

That said, between the 50,000 diets I have been on and the other billion I have studied and read about, there are some simple commonalities. These are listed in no specific order.

Healthful	Harmful
Water	*Soda (regular or diet)*
Fresh vegetables	*Refined sugars*
Fresh fruits	*Hydrogenated fats*
Healthy fats	*Excessive eating*
Protein	
Eating in moderation	
Unrefined Carbohydrates	

The good news is there is more on the healthful side than the harmful side! The challenge is to discover the proper balance of those healthful foods that work for you. Without question, whatever answer you find, a study will have been done to support and to discredit that answer. Still, we have to start someplace right?

Healthy eating does not require math, a PhD, case studies, expert advice or a kitchen full of expensive gadgets. All you need is a commitment to consume real food, eat to serve your body and a wiliness to make mistakes along the way. That's it.

If you are struggling with severe health concerns or if you are just curious, there are tests that will illuminate allergies, deficiencies and imbalances. However, if you seek to simply improve your general health; perhaps have more energy, achieve a healthy weight, have clear skin; giving up the crap and preparing home cooked, real food is a great place to start. Start drinking more pure, clean water and you will really be on to something.

To find your starting place, I suggest you make some lists. On the next page you will see 3 columns: 1) Foods you eat, 2) Emotion/feeling around that food 3) Nutritious or not? Take some time and fill in the columns. Once you make your lists, look for patterns. Do you notice that you tend toward a certain food when you are feeling stressed. Do you eat mostly nutritious foods and then binge on junk when you are tired?

Look up some of the foods and see what the experts say about them. For years we were told not to eat butter, now people put it in their coffee. Eggs good/eggs bad. Soy good/ soy bad. It's tough! Also consider how foods make you feel. Broccoli may be healthy but if it makes you bloated and causes you discomfort, you may want to avoid it, at least for awhile. This exercise helps us use our experience and preferences as research so we can develop our own way of eating. We need to stop thinking that we have failed at meeting our health goals because we could not stick to a plan. If we take responsibility for our health and do what works for us, we have to stick to because it is just what we do.

Foods you Eat	How do you feel when you eat these foods and/ or why do you consume them?	Nutritious? Yes/No/DK
Broccoli	*I love this stuff. Use it as a carrier for sauce and sometimes over do it.*	*Y*
Potato chips	*Salty, crunchy. Eat when I am stressed – always eat too much*	*N*
Hamburgers	*Good source of protein. Easy choice when eating out. Have to order without bun or French fries.*	*DK (don't know)*

How did that go? What did you learn?

See if you can identify 3 foods that you currently consume that you think are not serving you.

1)

2)

3)

What foods do you like that do serve you but you don't eat as often as you would like?

1)

2)

3)

Feel free to make up your own categories and develop your own ways of figuring out the best sources of nutrition for yourself. Some people like to keep a food journal. There are also several apps available. A word of caution about the apps; they tend to focus on calories. While calories are important, I suggest you focus on fueling your body and not worry about calories. Being mindful of your portions is usually enough to keep you on track if you are eating nutrient dense foods.

Why Cook

Many people, organizations and industries would like us to believe that eating is a science. Granted, the biology of how our body uses food is science; eating is, however, an art. We should experiment with food as an artist experiments with colors and techniques. As we discover new things, we work towards creating our own masterpieces.

As I stated, we eat for 2 reasons; to fuel our bodies and for pleasure. The key is to find the proper balance. What combinations and choices will provide your body with the best fuel and most pleasure. As the exercise above illustrates, you can learn what is working and what is not if you pay attention to your body, do a little research and apply what you have learned. You will know what changes you need to make to thrive no matter where you are in your life.

Food is fun, cooking is therapeutic and eating is pleasurable. We eat every day. Feeling bad about something we do everyday makes it tough to be happy. When we diet, we automatically label food as good and bad and then transfer those labels to ourselves when we eat them or even think about eating them. It's so silly.

Think about this statement. "I was so bad last night. I ate ice cream." Really? Is that "bad"? I say no, it is not "bad". It is not even necessarily unhealthy. Eating a pint of chocolate, chocolate chip, by yourself in front of the TV at midnight certainly does not serve your body; a scoop of ice cream at a picnic with your family is another story.

Once I stopped labeling my food as good or bad and removed the right and wrong attitude towards food I magically felt free to enjoy it and therefore stopped obsessing over it! Talk about taking a weight off!

Outside of allergies and health conditions, if you are consuming mostly whole foods that are responsibly sourced, you are on the right path. The only "bad" foods are the crap* (sorry, but it really is crap) that the food companies call food. It's not even bad food because it is not food; it is, well, crap!

Cooking at home is one way to guarantee you know what you are eating. The challenges may be you don't know how to cook, you don't feel you have time to cook or you don't have confidence in cooking healthy meals that taste good so you rely on packaged foods. These concerns are easy to address.

Just as with eating, cooking is mostly an art. Making healthy food taste good becomes easier with practice. Keep in mind that "good", as with art, is...well, a matter of taste. What one person raves about may cause another to head for the hot sauce. (Yes, this is how my husband lets me know a concoction is not on the "keeper" list.) Therefore, when it comes to cooking, the best place to start is the kitchen (ha...I bet you knew that...see you are a better cook than you knew!).

Start with something simple and remember that if you don't love it, you can make changes next time or just don't make it again. It's only one meal out of thousands you will make. You (and your fellow diners) will recover. My mom always told me, "Just keep doing stuff until you find something you like." I think that is good advice.

This book is intended as a guide for you to gain confidence and develop your own style in the kitchen. The more you cook and experiment; the more success you will have and the healthier you will become. Whether you have decided to embrace a healthy lifestyle out of need or desire, you will refine your approach in time.

The number of amazing cookbooks, recipe blogs and videos available is mind blowing. Honestly, I get overwhelmed by it. People with a full range of experience, cultural backgrounds and takes on great food are at your finger tips. Once you know you can prepare a simple nourishing meal, you can take it to the next level and start experimenting with new ingredients, techniques and flavor profiles.

The Recipes of Success

Once upon a time, people lived to eat and ate to live quite literally. Today, few of us depend on the daily catch, the gatherings of the day or the meager morsels the elders scrape together. For the most part, we can eat something whenever we want. Whether that something qualifies as food is another story. I won't get preachy (at least on in this book) about the state of food in our country, however I will say that not being dependent on prepackage foods as your source of daily sustenance is a HUGE step in reclaiming your health and happiness.

In other words, learning to cook simple meals from real food, everyday, is essential. Start here and the rest will fall into place. You don't need 45,000 cookbooks or 2 years of training to make a nutritious meal. You don't need a kitchen full of fancy gadgets to prepare or cook your food. Start with fresh food, a knife and a stove and you are ready to rock.

That is what the recipes in this book are about. They will set you up for success when it comes to feeding yourself and your loved ones real, flavorful, enjoyable food. Begin by simplifying your approach and attitude around food and making a meal, then if you want to take it to the next level, you will have the time and energy to get fancy.

Most people eat the same 12 things over and over again. I don't know where I read that but it really stuck with me and ever since, I have observed it to be true over and over again. Every time we go to my mom's house, we have grilled chicken and every time we like it. I make pancakes and bacon whenever my son has a sleepover. His friends ask for it every time. If we don't have tacos at least once every 2 weeks, I think the world may actually stop spinning on its axis. Those familiar flavors and experiences ground us and make us feel safe. To me, it makes sense to make our comfort foods in a way that also provides sound nutrition.

Don't get me wrong, getting stuck in a rut is not the answer either. Variety and experimenting with new foods is just as important. About once, sometimes twice a week, I will try something new. Sometimes it goes well, sometimes not so well. Once you get the handle on the basics, the kitchen is your studio and the plate your palette for your next masterpiece. Delicious food will flow from you and new ideas will come to you in the middle of the night…or not. Either way, once you start to own these recipes, coming up with new stuff will become easier.

Another consideration is the meal components or what I call your Go To Elements. Traditionally we had the basic 4 food groups. Then we had a pyramid and now I believe we are on a sectored MY Plate. Let's explore the concept of what we need at meal time further.

The Plate and Beyond

My intention is to not get all sciencey in this book and so I won't bore you with macro and micro nutrients or the differences between proteins, fats and carbohydrates. There are tons of books out there that will break that down for you. What I will say, is eating a variety of foods offers a good way to ensure you are getting all the stuff your body needs to function and thrive. Eliminating foods that you know to be over processed, contain artificial ingredients and /or come from questionable sources is a key to getting healthy and happy. Finally, as we have demonstrated, taking the time to understand what foods work best for your body is a valuable investment.

Once I cleaned up my diet, lost weight and was feeling pretty good I still felt "off". I struggle to explain it but I had brain fog almost always, my belly would bother me and I would wake up feeling like I drank a bottle of wine even if I hadn't. I was irritable and my skin broke out regularly. I went to allopathic doctors, naturopathic doctors and integrative doctors and each had their own theory, but none of them figured it out. It was when I went back over my mental log of diets and remembered feeling better when I was on the Atkins diet. The diet severely restricts carbohydrates and although I did not find everything in the approach to meet my needs, I did feel better so I decided to cut down on carbs and cut out wheat.

As a good (half) Italian girl, this was not easy. This was before the gluten free craze really hit so there were very few gluten free options at the local pizza joint and gluten free pasta tasted like wall paper paste, but...boy did I feel better. That was 3 years ago. Now, eating wheat free is just what I do and I eat meals with my family and friends without any stress. Here's how I do it.

THE ELEMENTS

I prepare the same meal for 4 people despite varying ages, tolerances and nutritional needs. I thrive on lower carb, wheat free meals throughout the day. My 9 year old and husband eat very little in the morning and then have a big dinner. The little guy is 6 years younger (if you are doing math, I had him at 41) and he eats a breakfast made for a 300 pound football player and a huge lunch and then is pretty much done come dinner. They all are thin and need lots of healthy calories to keep up their energy and mood levels.

We are allivores (I think I made that word up - I mean we eat everything) and so most of our meals contain a good amount of protein, veggies, and a carbohydrate. We also eat plenty of healthy fats. The kids eat fruit daily while my husband and I have fruit on occasion.

Keeping the elements in each meal simple allows each person to customize to their needs and tastes. This works well for picky eaters, young eaters and mixed company. If cooking for your family, you will learn what flavors work for everyone as individual palates mature and adapt to the healthier foods so you will be able to infuse more of these flavors into the foods. And remember, simple does not mean plain or boring.

The recipes in this book are nutritious on their own and even more so when brought together in as a meal. For the most part, I see starches, pasta, potatoes, rice and other grains as a base for sauces or other elements of the meal. I reserve fruits for snacks, condiments, dessert and occasionally breakfast. Since I limit my intake of starches and want to encourage my family to eat more veggies, I often include a starchy and non-starchy element, a raw veggie and a protein at each meal. For example, if we are having spaghetti for dinner, I will serve pasta (sometimes gluten free, sometimes not) a hot vegetable (usually broccoli or zucchini ribbons which are my favorite base for sauce and my oldest son devours so I have to make sure I have enough for the rest of us) some sliced cucumbers or a Caesar salad, meatballs and sauce.

The elements I look to include at each meal are:

1. Protein
2. Raw Vegetable or Salad
3. Hot Vegetable
4. Grain, Pasta or Potato
5. Sauce or Dip

Breakfast is an exception to this as time is an issue. I focus on protein at breakfast and often offer a whole fruit or smoothie for the kids. We also shake things up and have dinner for breakfast. Sometimes if I am running late, while I am packing lunch I will give the kids their lunch for breakfast and they think I am such a rebel!

VEGETARIAN/VEGAN AND RAW FOOD PLANS

Before we move on, I will briefly address plant based diets. Most of the recipes can be adapted to meet the needs of vegetarians and I have included some soy based proteins. Eating a healthy vegetarian diet is very doable and, for some people, a superior way to eat. The environmental and humanitarian aspects of this way of eating appeal to many people as well. I encourage you to take the time to understand how at attain proper nutrition if you choose to eliminate all animal based protein. Again, it is more than possible to thrive on a plant based diet as long as you know what foods to consume.

That said, I lived a vegetarian lifestyle for 10 years and I did not take the time to learn how to eat properly and suffered the consequences of an imbalanced diet. I now know a solely plant based diet does not work for me and I have chosen to include quality animal proteins. Since this book is based on how I genuinely prepare food, it reflects this preference.

ADJUSTING TO LOW CARBOHYDRATE/PALEO (LC)

For me, the pendulum swung hard. I went from being a vegetarian to including chicken and fish to going essentially Paleo, which focuses on animal protein, low carbohydrate vegetables and healthy fats. I am not strict. I do have dairy and potatoes on occasion. I splurge on corn chips when we go out for Mexican. The only absolute restriction I have made is gluten for the reasons I stated previously. I have come to this approach over time by listening to my body and considering my lifestyle. I am able to eat well, stay healthy and not obsess over what I can and cannot eat. If I feel I have put on some weight, I lower the starches and dairy. It's not a big deal and I don't beat myself up. I don't let things spin out of control on either gaining or losing. I did that for too long and it is just not healthy!

I have become quite savvy when it comes to creating low starch elements. I will get into that more specifically: what I want to point out here is that by using the strategies that follow, I literally don't worry about making separate food for myself or not being able to eat something whether I am at home, out and about or dining at a friend's house.

THE PRESENTATION

In addition to learning to create new recipes, you can get creative on how you present a meal. For example, weekday scrambled eggs turn into weekend breakfast bar. Same basic element presented a new way with a few added components to increase nutritional variety and excitement.

I offer meals using 3 different approaches; the plated meal, the build your own bar and the Dibs & Dabs. Each as its own benefits and can ease meal time stress in an instant. Let me explain.

THE PLATE

This is the traditional approach toward a meal. I prepare 3-4 elements for each plate: a protein, 2 veggies and a starch. I usually bring the elements to the table and we plate them together, which allows people to determine how much of what and where they want it on their plate. A few things to keep in mind:

1. While choices are presented, each person can only choose from what is on the table which spares you from needing to make more than 1 meal.
2. If you are feeding your family, keep in mind that children will love and hate a certain food within the same week. They also will refuse to eat certain foods just to drive you

crazy. That's okay. Just keep offering healthy options and eventually, if that is all that is available, they will eat.

3. Dips and sauces often help encourage people to try things. Having little bowls or ramekins on the table for people to keep a sauce from migrating on their plate can eliminate wasted food and makes things fun as well.

4. Again, with children, "refusal without trying" is not standard operating procedure. While it is not worth fighting about, if you create the expectation that everyone should at least try things before refusing them, it helps kids (and picky eaters) discover flavors and broaden their palate.

When it comes to how much of what, the ratios are not crucial as long as they are having some of each of the elements most of the time. My oldest son and I love salad and hot veggies. My little guy is a protein and raw veggie fiend. My husband eats everything in balance. My folks eat much less these days so their portions tend to be smaller. The tips above encourage variety and experimentation so in the scheme of things, balance is often achieved.

I think of things in a 3 day versus 3 meal rotation. Some days I just don't want raw vegetables – so I don't eat them, knowing that I will probably have a salad for lunch within the next day or two. I provide the same flexibility to my kids. It saves a lot of stress and reduces "food issues", both of which undermine your wellbeing.

BUILD YOUR OWN BAR (byob)

I think the trending term for this approach would be the "deconstructed" meal. It is fun and is my favorite presentation. I love observing the combinations people come up with on their own. The possibilities are endless and you can offer as few or as many options as you want. You can set the bar up on the table or you can line it up on the kitchen counter, make your meal and bring it to the table. Think about what will work for you and your diners.

The basic elements include a base and then toppings. Let's use the taco bar as an example:

Base Elements	Toppings

Base Elements

- Taco Shells
- Romaine Lettuce leaves (LC)
- Taco Meat (Ground Turkey, Ground Beef, Sliced Chicken, Beans, Crumble Tofu)

Toppings

- Shredded Cheese
- Diced Tomatoes
- Cilantro
- Salsas (Spicy, Mild, Fruit)
- Guacamole
- Beans (Black Bean, Refried)
- Olives
- Jalapeños

The key to success here is in the prep. You want the diner to be able to easily assemble their meal. All the elements need to be "ready to eat". It requires a little extra chopping but it pays off in the end.

Here's a list of ideas to get your creative juices flowing:

- Pizza Bar (have the crust pre-baked, let them top and just broil for 5 minutes. For easy low carb, I put some sautéed zucchini in a small oven safe dish, add my toppings and broil with the rest)
- Yogurt Bar (plain yogurt with fresh fruits, granola, nuts)
- Sandwich Bar (Low Carb – Salad Bar)
- Pasta Bar (different sauces, meats, cheeses…)

What can you come up with?

-
-

DIBs & DABs

The sophisticated way to refer to this is Tapas or Small Plates. I see it as a great way to clean out the fridge (shhh don't tell!) Okay, yes, this approach does lend itself to leftovers but it works well as a planned meal too. The main difference between this and the BYOB you don't have a base element. You can have a theme if you want but it is not necessary.

I like to do an expanded cheese and cracker DIBs & DABs on a lazy Sunday instead of doing a lunch. I'll put out a variety of meats and cheeses, olives, pickles, crackers and sliced veggies (LC) and dips. We just munch and watch movie or play a game.

How to Use This Book

This is YOUR book. I encourage you to write all over it.

When a famous person puts out a cookbook; they own the recipes and they expect and deserve credit. Since this is YOUR book, YOU get to take all the credit. You can scratch stuff out, write in the margins, tweak the recipes and best of all, add your own. I expect you to take credit for all the great recipes you create once you get in the kitchen and start experimenting for yourself.

This book is meant to be a guide and workbook. The more stains, notes and dog eared pages, the better. It belongs in your kitchen, not your coffee table.

1. The questions: Here you have the opportunity to gather information about yourself. Be honest and who knows what you will discover. You may choose to ignore them: this is YOUR book.

2. The recipe guides: room for personalization. (check out the sample entry on pg 30)
   a. There is space for you to change the quantity to the left of each ingredient
   b. There is space for you to change the ingredient to the right and above
   c. There is space for you to add ingredients below the list
   d. There is space for you to make notes where ever you see fit

3. Your recipes: Where you get to shine. (see pages 32-33)
   a. Title it – be descriptive, get creative and have some fun
   b. Write your description and share the story of how the recipe came about. This is a great way to start collecting memories for you and your family.
   c. Take a picture. You worked hard to create this masterpiece and it deserves to be photographed. Plus we all like cookbooks for the pictures right?
   d. List the ingredients in order of use
   e. Provide the directions.

Finally, be willing to tweak your own recipes as your cooking progresses.

Spinach and Walnut Pesto

This recipe came about when I was learning to cook in Boston. Traditional pesto is made with basil and pine nuts; however these ingredients can be hard to find and expensive so...we used fresh spinach and walnuts. The result is a delicious, healthy and affordable pesto. It also works great as a base for you to include additional herbs, greens and seasonings. The amount of oil you add will determine the thickness of your pesto. Think thick for spreads, a little more oil for a sauce on veggies or pasta and a touch more for a dip or dressing base.

Spinach and Walnut Pesto

Ingredients

1 bunch or 16oz bag		fresh spinach (baby or regular)
1/3 cup	½ cup	~~raw walnuts~~ (whole or pieces)
	1-2	cloves raw or roasted garlic
	½ cup	Parmesan (optional)
Add handful basil	½ cup +	extra virgin olive oil
Add ¼ tsp cayenne	TT	Salt

Directions

1. Make sure spinach is washed and drained (bagged spinach comes washed)
2. Place spinach and other herbs into food processor or blender. If it does not all fit, you many need to pulse a few times to decrease volume and continue to add and pulse until it all fits. *Use vitamix – add oil in bottom to get it going*
3. Add nuts and garlic. Pulse a few times to incorporate.
4. Remove pouring lid (make sure the main lid remains on) from your processor or blender.
5. Turn machine on and slowly pour in oil. Stop when desired consistency is achieved. You can add more oil for more a dip sauce or dressing.
6. Salt to taste.
7. If adding other dried spices, add them now and taste as you go.

1. If using regular spinach, simply tear leaves from center stem. Use baby spinach as is.

2. Whole nuts are often more expensive than pieces. Also feel free to experiment with other nuts such as cashews and macadamias.

3. If you prefer a mild garlic flavor use only one clove and/or use roasted garlic.

4. Pesto is delicious with or without the added cheese. You can substitute any hard cheese for the Parmesan (Asiago, Romano, aged nutritional or brewer's yeast for a non dairy version.

Your Notes:

Tried with cilantro and cumin, thumbs up from Joe but kids did not like.

Added fresh tomatoes – pulsed a few time in processors – Awesome!

Rita's Red Sauce

I took this recipe from what I can remember about cooking with my grandmother 30 years ago. She would start with fresh tomatoes and make her own bone broth. I have modernized the recipe and my Dad has given me his blessings. We love it over zucchini ribbons or rice pasta with fresh parmesan cheese..Delicious!

Rita's Red Sauce

Ingredients

4 lbs	Fresh tomatoes
½ cup	Fresh basil
1-2	Cloves raw or roasted garlic
½ cup	Tomato paste
½ cup +	Extra virgin olive oil
	Salt to taste

Directions

Steam tomatoes, peel and seed. Throw in blender with all the ingredients other than salt and olive oil. Simmer for 2 hours and tomatoes are completely broken down. Stir in olive oil and salt to taste.

Confidence in the Kitchen

I believe 3 core reasons to GET COOKING are:

- Sound Nutrition
- Elimination of Unnecessary Stress
- Joy in Your Home

I have stated my case for sound nutrition. You have to nourish your body in order for it to function. It is just that simple. We discussed the value of starting where you are, applying what you know and moving toward where you want to go one meal at a time. Let's move on to stress.

Stress is necessary. It helps us stay motivated, it helps us learn what is working in our lives and what it not and it helps us run away from lions if we find ourselves is such a situation. We can manage necessary stress if we begin to eliminate unnecessary stress. Without getting into brain function and the toll of stress on our bodies and the need to get rid of toxic people and all that stuff, let's just look at things we can control now and start there.

We can control what we put into our mouths. We can control how we choose what to put into our mouths and how we prepare what goes into our mouths. Meals should not be an added stress in our lives.

I know a lot of people advocate meal planning and this is a great idea! When I plan my meals I am less stressed; however planning meals totally stresses me out. I get caught up in the what format I should use and can I create a shopping list and do I have cumin or did I run out of cumin for that recipe. So, if you enjoy planning and want to plan your meals, you should do that, because it is a good tool. If you do not – all is not lost. I keep a standard grocery list of stuff I use all the time and I make sure I have it. I check out 1-2 new recipes each week and "plan" for them. I make some mental notes about what the week looks like and what I may do but I don't stress it and I always find a way to feed myself and my family.

That is why I advocate you find your Go To Elements, play around with some sauces and the presentation. Again, I say find what works for you and do it. Just be willing to let go of the "supposed to's " and do the "what works for you's".

If you cook for people other than yourself, it can become stressful. By embracing the presentation concepts and applying the techniques in this section, you will have the tools you need to make a healthy meal for everybody at the table without sacrificing how you want to eat.

As for joy in the home; whether you live alone, with roommates or your family, your home should be your sanctuary. Home is your safe and happy place. The place where all the unnecessary stress falls away and you can exhale. Granted, not every moment is total bliss, especially if you live with other people, however, the general sense that your home provides the space and energy you need to be at peace is important.

Part of creating that peace is to have mealtime be a time of joy. Whether you dine alone or with others, food is a grounding force that promotes the enjoyment of our own thoughts and the sharing of our thoughts with others. Create ceremony around at least a few meals a week and create traditions around fun ways to eat. Friday taco night or Sunday DIBs & DABs both become something that people look forward to having each week.

Okay, enough philosophy, on to the practical stuff. I am going to share some techniques that I use to simplify meal preparation while maximizing the nutrition. Check them out, try them, improve and customize them for yourself.

EQUIPMENT

Let's start with the equipment I use every day.

- **Stove and Oven** – Cooking is tough without something to cook on so, hot plate and toaster oven work. It need not be fancy, just able to get hot.

- **Good wooden cutting board** – I prefer wood over synthetic boards because they don't scratch as easily and therefore harbor fewer bacteria. I simply rinse my boards with eco friendly soap and hot water and then let them air dry. I do suggest you have a separate board for cutting meats and that you spray them down with undiluted white vinegar or a diluted bleach solution after washing.
- **Chefs' knife** – a chef's knife has a blade that extends beyond the handle for easy chopping. Several specialized knives exist and I am sure they work best for whatever they are intended, however I use a chef's knife 90% of the time and a paring knife the other 10%.
- **Food Processor/Blender** – I suggest you have at least one of the following. They are listed in order of priority. Throughout the recipes if I have used one of these gadgets, I simply use the word "processor" and you can use whichever you prefer or own.
    - **Food Processor:** this works best for chopping and blending foods. If I had to pick only one on this list, a traditional food processer would be it
    - **Vitamix or Blendtec:** These are high end blenders that do wonders with liquids. They are great if you want to emulsify (blend really, really well). I use my Vitamix when using nuts as a dairy substitute since it creates the best texture. Nice to have but not vital.
    - **Single Serve Blender:** Often known as the Bullet although there are many manufacturers. I use my bullet daily. I love it since it is small, easy to clean and does a good job. I can do almost everything in it from chopping to blending. It is limited because it is small so things like pesto and salsa do much better in the food processer. This is a great investment since they are affordable and handy.
    - **Blender:** Since I own the above 3 items, I rarely use my blender. It's a good tool to have if you do not own a Vitamix or Bullet. It is NOT a good substitute for the food processor as it does not chop well.
- **Sauce Pan** – This does not need to be fancy. Depending on how many people you cook for, you may need to use a 4 quart sauce pan. I use a 2 quart.

- **Steamer Basket** – I use a super inexpensive bamboo steamer basket. It came with 2 levels and I lost one so now I have only one and I manage most of the time. If I am steaming a lot of food, I will use my 5 quart Dutch oven with a wire colander and a lid.
- **Skillets** - I use these daily. I have owned the same cast iron pans for 20 years. They came in a set and they are all I use. I have a 5 inch, 8 inch and 10.5 inch skillet. I also have a 12 inch grill that I use for meats which I like but don't need. You don't have to use cast iron however, if you have old non-stick pans coated with Teflon, PLEASE replace them. They have new, eco friendly non-stick pans or, since I am going to show you how to keep food from sticking, why not invest in the cast iron? You can get a set of 3-5 pans for under a $100 and it is well worth it.

That's it! Yep. Granted, there is so much more you CAN and eventually should have; however, all of the recipes in this book were made by using these simple tools.

INGREDIENTS

When choosing ingredients, I follow some simple rules. If it is packaged, check the labels. My goal is to prepare REAL food that is a close to its whole state as possible. I am not a farmer, therefore I make compromises. My meat is butchered, my dairy rarely raw and my produce is not fresh from the vine that day. The compromises I make are manageable so I stick to my rules with rare exception because I know I am putting this stuff into my body 3 times a day. If it is laden with pesticides, chemicals and sugar, it does not serve or nourish me so I don't eat it.

- **Produce** (fruits and vegetables)
  - Fresh is best
  - Frozen works
  - Rarely canned (except tomatoes and beans)
  - Organic whenever possible
- **Meat**
  - Organic, grass fed is best

- o No hormones or antibiotics is a must
- o If processed (bacon, deli meats, sausages) the above + no added nitrites or nitrates, minimally processed.
- **Dairy**
  - o Organic, grass fed is best
  - o No hormones or antibiotics is a must
  - o No added sugars (yogurt)
  - o If it as more than 3 ingredients...why?
- **Starches** (pasta, rice, grains, potatoes)
  - o Organic is best
  - o No seasoning packets
- **Nuts and Seeds**
  - o Organic is best
  - o Natural Food store bulk is good
  - o Avoid store bought, prepackaged, roasted, salted or flavored varieties
- **Packaged Foods** (cookies, crackers, mixes, canned tomatoes and beans, condiments etc)
  - o Organic is best
  - o No trans fats
  - o No artificial sweeteners
  - o No weird preservatives
  - o If more than 5 ingredients, do I really need/want it
- **Fats – IMPORTANT** – I eat a lot of fat so it is essential that I do my best to use it properly. The information out there on which are the "good" fats is just as convoluted as the rest of the nutritional advice; however, one thing that is common and consistent in the literature is the impact heating has on fat. To summarize, it is not a good idea to expose oils to high heat especially for an extended time. When it comes to cooking with fat, I am cautious. Here is what I use and how I use it.
  - o **Unsalted Grass Fed Butter** – cooking, baking and flavor at the end of heating

- Ghee – this is butter that has had the milk solids removed. It is an excellent choice for cooking especially if you are dairy free.
- **Unrefined Extra Virgin Cold Pressed Coconut Oil** – baking and cooking
- **Extra Virgin Cold Pressed Olive Oil** – Salad dressing, flavoring – NEVER heated
- **Toasted Sesame Oil** – Added flavor and occasionally for cooking. A little goes a long way.
- **Avocados, Nuts and Seeds** – Raw, occasionally toasted nuts

TECHNIQUES

I have been through a lot when it comes to food and yet I still love it. Some days I love it more than others and there are those days where the thought of making yet another meal makes me want to weep. Since I eat well most days, when I hit one of *these* days, I don't really cook I heat things up. Apple Chicken sausage with baked beans, sliced cucumbers and a tossed salad it is! No guilt, no stress and still healthy because I read labels and look at the ingredients.

Most days I cook. Cooking truly is an art and so many creative tools, techniques, tips and tricks are available. What I am sharing is the tip of the iceberg and I hope these techniques will act as the catalyst for you to discover more. Here are some techniques I use. Keep these abbreviations in mind as I will use them in the recipes.

Cold Grease (CG) – Take a small amount of butter, ghee or coconut oil and rub the skillet as if you were greasing a pan for baking. Heat the pan. As soon as it looks shiny, it is ready for food. Watch that it does not smoke. Add water or additional fat if needed or if called for in recipe.

Water Cook (WC) – Gradually add small amounts of water to food while it is cooking to prevent food sticking and to foster cooking. This method essentially steams the food. It works well with veggies, eggs and burgers. I do not use this method with other meats.

Steam Tower (ST)– This is how I make my starch base and my non-starch base in 1 fell swoop. Simply boil your water, add your starch and return to boil. Once you are back up to boil, turn your stove down so you still see bubbles but it is not boiling over. Place your non-starch veggies into the steamer, put on the lid and place on the pot. After 5 minutes check your veggies and remove or leave on until your desired texture is achieve.

To Taste (TT) – This term applies to how done you want something or how seasoned. For example: cook your steak TT means to the temperature you prefer (Rare, Medium, Well), do you like your pasta soft or al dente, veggies crisp or more cooked down. A general rule of thumb to consider is, the more cooked, the less nutrients.

To Taste for seasonings refers to how spicy, salty, peppery etc do you like your food.

Parchment Lined Foil – when using aluminum foil, place a piece of unbleached parchment between your food and the foil. This avoids the metallic taste, food sticking to the foil and any leaching of the aluminum into your food.

Crushed Garlic – I use a lot of garlic. I believe garlic adds depth to almost any savory dish. To peel, I use the crush method. You simply place your knife over a single clove of garlic and smash it with your fists cracking open the peel and making it easier to pop the clove out.

I use garlic 3 ways.

1. **Raw** – crushed, minced and in.
    a. *This provides a powerful garlic taste and can get a bit spicy if you use a lot.*
2. **Boiled** – crushed and in the pot. I sometimes remove the garlic but usually I incorporate it into the recipe. Think mashed potatoes, mashed cauliflower and tomato sauce.
    a. *This provides a mellow flavor and infuses the other ingredients for greater depth.*
3. **Roasted** – leave the garlic in the peel, place in aluminum foil lined with parchment paper, seal and roast in oven (toaster oven) at 350 for 45-60 minutes. You can then peel and use or put into a container and store in the refrigerator for up to 2 weeks.
    a. *This provides a mellow rich flavor and can be substituted for all or some of the raw garlic called for in a recipe if you want a more subtle garlic flavor or want to avoid the spiciness of using all raw.*

Go Slow, Taste/Test as you Go (GSTG) – This concept can save a recipe. Adding too much of something can take a meal that was "almost there" to "yuck" in a flash: too much salt, too much vinegar, too much water when using the Water Cooking method can make a happy cook less happy. Just add slowly, and taste it or watch it for minute before you pour more in. Keep in mind – *Testing is NOT eating.* This is the Golden Rule for not overeating when you cook.

This is where your book begins.

Place your picture here and write your dedication.

Dedication

RECIPES

These are my GO TO recipes and are based on serving 4.

I make these over and over again; sometimes tweaking them based on what ingredients I have on hand, what flavors I am in the mood for or just because I feel like it. Focus on the basics and then let your imagination take control of the flavors and combinations.
Soon you will have your own
GO TO Recipes.

Master Spice Blend (MSB)

Developing a blend of spices that you can rely on to give your food great flavor is a simple way to streamline your seasoning process. I use this blend endlessly. Sometimes I change the ratios or leave out the salt depending on what I am seasoning. I use it alone and I use it in conjunction with other herbs and spices.

Master Spice Blend (MSB)

Ingredients

1 part   Everyday Seasoning Blend

1 part   Garlic Powder

            Pink Himalayan Salt

Directions

1. Sprinkle on meat to season before cooking.
2. Add to sauces for flavor enhancement.
3. Season veggies and eggs after cooking.
4. The list goes on….

1. This blend comes in a grinder and contains:
   a. Sea salt
   b. Mustard Seed
   c. Black Pepper
   d. Coriander
   e. Dried Onion
   f. Dried Garlic
   g. Chili Pepper
2. When you develop your own blend, I suggest you minimize the salt and anything too spicy. You can always add more. This is your base to use on any and everything.

Your Notes:

YOUR
Master Spice Blend
HERE!

_____

Ingredients

Directions

It's all in the

SAUCE

*You can transform plain ole anything into
something delicious with the right sauce.
Lettuce becomes a Caesar, chicken becomes a favorite,
and veggies get eaten. I have included a variety
of sauces that can be adopted to meet
the tastes and needs of most diners.
Play around with different herbs, spices and
combinations. Try mixing the Pesto with a vinaigrette or
dollop some on the Tomato Sauce instead of cheese.*

(Asian) Vinaigrette

A good dressing makes a good salad great. Of course, vinaigrettes also make wonderful marinades; add zip to steamed veggies and act as a simple dip for fresh crudities. To top it all off, vinaigrettes are quick and easy to make. This recipe has an Asian flair; however the Tip Box has the basic principles to follow for any vinaigrette.

Asian Vinaigrette

Ingredients

½ cup	Olive oil
2 teaspoons	Toasted Sesame Oil
1-2 teaspoons	Ginger/Ginger Juice
¼ cup	Rice Wine Vinegar
1 Tablespoon chopped	Cilantro
1 Tablespoon chopped	Scallion

1. The key to good vinaigrette is ratios. 1 part acid to 2 parts oil is a good rule of thumb.
2. Acids include your vinegars, lemon/lime juice and other fruit juices.
3. You can adjust this ratio with a bit of water but go slow and add as you go.

Your Notes:

Directions

1. You can mix your vinaigrette by hand in a bowl or put everything in your processor and give it a whirl. If you choose to do it by hand, you will need to mince your herbs. If using a processor just place the herbs in first to chop and then toss in the rest of the ingredients.
2. Mix until the ingredients have come together and the oil is not longer separated.

Dairy Free Creamy Dressing

The base for most creamy dressings contain dairy. This one is made with raw cashews and is so creamy you would never know it's high in protein, healthy fats and fiber and completely dairy free. The trick is to soak the nuts and make sure you puree them well. Once you discover this unique dressing, you may never use store bought ranch again.

Dairy Free Creamy Dressing

Ingredients

½ cup	Soaked Cashews
1-2 Tbsp	Apple cider vinegar or lemon juice
1 cup	Fresh herbs (loosely packed)
1 small or ½ large clove	Garlic
TT	Salt
1/4 cup + TT	Water to emulsify

Directions

Throw everything except the salt into your processor with a ¼ cup water and blend well. Slowly add more water until the desired texture is achieved. The Vitamix works great for this dressing.

1. Soak your cashews in fresh water for about 6 hours or overnight. Drain and rinse before using.
2. Cashews work well because of their texture. You can use macadamias or brazil nuts with a similar result.
3. You can use seeds in place of nuts if allergies are a concern; I find sunflower seeks work well.
4. You can eliminate the acid in this recipe if desired.
5. The herbs are up to you. Dill and parsley both make a fresh flavor and work well as the primary herb mixed with other herbs.
6. You can skip the garlic, but I would not skip the garlic and the acid. Your dressing will taste flat.

Your Notes:

Chimichurri

This sauce is both versatile and nutritious. Full of powerful leafy green herbs, garlic and onions, this is a great "green smoothy" without all the fruit sugars. A traditional Argentinean condiment for steak, Chimichurri is also amazing on fish, chicken and on sandwiches. It adds wonderful balance drizzles over an earthy bean soup. Here I put it on my turkey and cheese green leaf sandwich. It was so good I made another one!

Chimichurri

Ingredients

1 cup loosely packed	Flat leaf parsley
1 / 4 cup	Fresh herbs (oregano works well)
2-3	cloves raw or roasted garlic
1 small	shallot (sub 2T chive or onion)
2 Tbsp	Lemon juice
2 Tbsp	Red wine or other mild vinegar
½ cup +	Olive Oil
TT	Red Pepper
TT	Black Pepper
TT	Salt

1. Feel free to experiment with the base herb. Cilantro, spinach or a combo of fresh leafy herbs
2. The amount of lemon juice and vinegar can be played with as well. Steak can bare more acidity whereas if you are using on fish or chicken you may want to use less.
3. This is meant to be a spicy sauce. You can even use a little fresh jalapeño or habanera here or to meet the palate of your dinners, you can eliminate all the heat and just put some red pepper flakes on the table.

Your Notes:

Directions

1. Place all ingredients into a processor and pulse to desired texture.

NOTE: Traditionally, Chimichurri has a chunky texture. I tend to puree it more, as shown in the picture, because my family and I prefer the smoother texture. I also like to drizzle it as a condiment and find the puree more versatile.

Spinach and Walnut Pesto

This recipe came about when I was learning to cook in Boston. Traditional pesto is made with basil and pine nuts; however these ingredients can be hard to find and expensive so...we used fresh spinach and walnuts. The result is a delicious, healthy and affordable pesto. It also works great as a base for you to include additional herbs, greens and seasonings. The amount of oil you add will determine the thickness of your pesto. Think thick for spreads, a little more oil for a sauce on veggies or pasta and a touch more for a dip or dressing base.

Spinach and Walnut Pesto

Ingredients

1 bunch or 16oz bag	fresh spinach (baby or regular)
½ cup	raw walnuts (whole or pieces)
1-2	cloves raw or roasted garlic
½ cup	Parmesan (optional)
½ cup +	extra virgin olive oil
	Salt to taste

Directions

1. Make sure spinach is washed and drained (bagged spinach comes washed)
2. Place spinach and other herbs into food processor or blender. If it does not all fit, you many need to pulse a few times to decrease volume and continue to add and pulse until it all fits.
3. Add nuts and garlic. Pulse a few times to incorporate.
4. Remove pouring lid (make sure the main lid remains on) from your processor or blender.
5. Turn machine on and slowly pour in oil. Stop when desired consistency is achieved. You can add more oil for more a dip sauce or dressing.
6. Salt to taste.
8. If adding other dried spices, add them now and taste as you go.

Stuff to add: Sundried tomatoes, fresh herbs (basil, cilantro, oregano, dill, parsley), cayenne pepper, cumin. Just remember to think over your flavor profile, start with a little and taste as you go.

---

1. If using regular spinach, simply tear leaves from center stem. Use baby spinach as is.
2. Whole nuts are often more expensive than pieces. Also feel free to experiment with other nuts such as cashews and macadamias.
3. If you prefer a mild garlic flavor use only one clove and/or use roasted garlic.
4. Pesto is delicious with or without the added cheese. You can substitute any hard cheese for the Parmesan (Asiago, Romano, aged Provolone, or try nutritional or brewer's yeast for a non dairy version.

Your Notes:

No, No, No Caesar

This no egg, no dairy no fuss version has all the creamy, salty, rich flavors expected in Caesar dressing including the benefits of anchovies such as protein, Omega 3 fatty acids and calcium. My family loves this stuff and it is a great way to dress up any green leaf salad.

No, No, No Caesar

Ingredients

2 oz tin	Whole anchovies filets in olive oil
1-2 Tbsp TT	Fresh squeezed lemon
1-2	Cloves raw or roasted garlic
2 Tbsp	Water
1-2 Tbsp	Mayo (optional)
1-2 Tbsp	Parmesan cheese

1. You can substitute any hard cheese for the Parmesan (Asiago, Romano, aged Provolone)
2. If some but not all of your diners are dairy free, skip the cheese in the dressing and put it on the table for people add.
3. Feel free to add more lemon, and or substitute lime juice for a nice twist.

Your Notes:

Directions

1. Put the anchovies with oil into your processor (reserving a few for garnish if you desire)
2. Add lemon and garlic
3. Process until smooth
4. Add water and process until completely blended.
5. Taste – if too salty, add more water but remember this is going to dress a salad so the salt will dissipate.
6. Add cheese if desired and pulse until incorporated
7. Stir in mayo for a creamier dressing.

Add ins: Add a little cayenne pepper for some kick. Black and white pepper are nice additions. Herbs such as dill or tarragon add color and flavor as well.

Good for ya Guacamole

When it comes to healthy fat, avocados lead the pack. Creamy and green; what more can you ask of a single fruit (yes it is a fruit – I am sure!). Guacamole is commonly seen at your favorite Mexican restaurant however this condiment is also wonderful with eggs, as a spread and as a dip. You can play with spices and textures. Whatever you choose to do with it, adding more avocados into your routine is a healthy move.

Good for ya Guac

Ingredients

2-3	Ripe Avocados
1-2 cloves	Garlic (raw or roasted) minced
¼ small	Onion (diced small)
½ fresh or 1 Tbsp	Lime Juice
TT	Salt
TT	Cayenne pepper (optional)

Directions

You can make this by hand or in your processor. If you use your processor, remember to pulse the ingredients for a courser texture or you can puree for a smooth texture.

1. Place the flesh of the avocado in a bowl and mash.
2. Add in remaining ingredients through salt and combine until desired texture is achieved.
3. Season TT.

Stuff to add: Fresh tomatoes, fresh herbs (basil, cilantro, oregano, dill, parsley), cayenne pepper, cumin.

You can also mix in yogurt for a light dip.

1. Making sure your avocado is ripe is key to a good guacamole. The outer skin should be a dark, almost black/green and have a slight give when gently squeezed.
2. Roasted garlic is great if you want to make more of a smooth mayo like spread.
3. Scallions can be substituted for onions.
4. Lemon can sub for lime.

Your Notes:

Supposed to be Mango Salsa

I talked about tweaking and here it is; a true tweak. I planned to have BYOB Taco's for dinner and was gathering my salsa makings. I opened the freezer to snag my mango and...no mangos. I could have gone without a fruit salsa except I needed to take a picture! This book represents real life. Just getting in the kitchen and cooking so...here we have cantaloupe salsa and may I just say...delicious! A successful tweak.

Supposed to be Mango Salsa

Ingredients

½	Cantaloupe peeled & deseeded
½	Red onion
1-2 Tbsp (TT)	Lime juice
¼ cup	Cilantro chopped
TT	Salt
TT	Pepper (Black)
TT	Cayenne pepper

Directions

Salsa is fun and versatile. You can use fresh, canned or even green tomatoes in this recipe. I, of course would add garlic for a tomato salsa although I do not like the garlic with the fruit salsas. Whatever you try, the basic directions are the same.

1. If using garlic, red or white onion, place in the processor and pulse to chop. If using scallions or chives skip this step and go to step 2.
2. Put herbs and fruit or tomatoes into your processor and pulse a few times to integrate but keep chunky.
3. Add lime and spices and pulse again. Taste and adjust.
4. Continue to pulse until desired texture is achieved. If you reach your don't want to over puree your salsa, you can simply pour your salsa into a bowl and stir in the lime and seasonings.

Add ins and ideas:

- Try using fresh hot peppers like jalapenos, habaneras or chipotle to add flavor and heat. GSTG!
- Cumin, cinnamon, chili powder, smoked paprika all add flavor.

1. For the Mango version, use 3 fresh mangos, peeled and removed from pit or 3 cups frozen mango – thawed.

2. You can use any form of onion, sweet, white, scallions or chives. All offer a subtle shift in flavor and texture.

3. The lime juice provides balance to the sweetness of the fruit. It also provides the authentic flavor of a salsa. You can substitute lemon.

4. Cilantro is a traditional herb for many Hispanic dishes. Basil is a great compliment to the fruit salsas and would have been excellent with the cantaloupe.

5. The black pepper completed the flavor profile with the cantaloupe. White pepper has a unique flavor and is worth trying.

Your Notes:

Thai Peanut Sauce

This exotic, dairy free sauce is good both warmed and chilled. I use it warmed over chicken, mixed with pasta or veggies. You can also make a cold noodle dish with this sauce or use it as dip for veggies. The coconut milk provides healthy fats, great texture and a rich and slightly sweet flavor. Experiment with different nut butters, herbs and spices for a delicious and versatile sauce.

Thai Peanut Sauce

Ingredients

1 cup	Coconut milk
¼ cup	Peanut Butter
1	Clove Garlic
1 Tbsp	Cilantro
1 Tbsp	Soy Sauce or Braggs Aminos
1 Tbsp	Ginger Juice
1	Soaked Date
1 tsp	Lime

1. You can substitute Sunbutter for Peanut if you have nut allergies or try different butters to change the flavor
2. Soy Sauce contains wheat. You can use Tamari, Braggs Aminos or Coconut Aminos, all of which are wheat free
3. Ginger juice is a wonderful time saver and is available in most Health Food stores or you can check the Asian section of your supermarket. You can sub 1 inch fresh ginger.
4. The date provides a natural sweetness and fiber. You can use 1 Tbsp of sugar or maple syrup as well

Your Notes:

Directions

1. Pop everything into your processor and blend.

Garnish with chopped scallions or chives for a good flavor balance and color.

Harvest Chutney

Chutney is often served with Indian dishes and is a blend of sweet and savory. This Chutney pairs well with the MoKa Java Pork recipe. It offers just enough sweet that the kids will like it without tasting like dessert and makes for an interesting topping on a piece of sharp cheddar or even vanilla ice cream.

Harvest Chutney

Ingredients

2	Apples diced
2	Pears diced
½	Orange
1-2	Onions diced
½ cup	Raisins
1-2 Tbsp TT	Apple Cider Vinegar
½ tsp	Cinnamon
TT	Black Pepper

Directions

1. You can decide whether to peel or not peel your apples and pears before you dice them. I do not. Also, making the pieces consistent in size will produce a smoother texture while varying the size will make for chunkier chutney.
2. CG a sauce pan and add onions. WC them until they become soft.
3. Add a little water to sauce pan and add your fruits. Cook over medium heat until fruits soften. About 10 minutes
4. Taste. Add 1 Tbsp vinegar, and stir in. Taste again. Keep adding until you get the tang you want.
5. Add your spices.

Chutney can be served warm or cold. Place in a glass container and store in fridge for up to 3 weeks.

1. You can mix the variety of apples and pears any way you wish. All apples, all pears, mix it up.
2. Try stone fruits like peaches and nectarines.
3. You can substitute any citrus here – Clementine, Grapefruit, Tangerine.
4. Try other dried fruits. Cherries, cranberries and currents taste wonderful.
5. Adjust the amount of cider vinegar to taste after you have cooked down your fruit so you can decide what balance works for you.
6. I used pumpkin spice blend here which added some clove and nutmeg which was nice.

Your Notes:

Tomato Sauce Gone Simple

I am Italian and I did not know how to make sauce. How can this be you ask? Well, my mom, whom I love, is not Italian so...no sauce   A true sauce, or gravy as the Italians call it, can easily take all day. This sauce takes less than an hour at most. It's a good little sauce and one that you can proudly add to your meatballs, pasta, and pizza or veggie parmesan.

Tomato Sauce Gone Simple

Ingredients

15 oz can	Tomatoes (Crushed, plain, no salt)
1/2	Small onion, diced
2-3	Crushed cloves garlic
2 sprigs	Fresh herbs (oregano, basil)
2 Tbsp	Olive oil
TT	Salt
TT	Red Pepper (optional)
1 + cups for SYV	Beef broth (chix or veggie)

Directions

To avoid using sugar in this sauce, caramelize the onions, and keep the garlic intact while cooking. Follow these 2 steps and the rest is up to you.

1. CG your pan and heat over medium high heat.
2. Dice the onion so the pieces are fairly small. This allows them to cook down faster and melt into the sauce. SYV with broth. Beef broth will offer a richer taste; chicken and veggie are okay as well. Water will yield a less robust flavor. Cook down until onions are soft and brown.
3. Add your tomatoes, garlic and herbs and cover. Turn down stove and simmer for 30 minutes. Check occasionally to make sure the tomatoes are not too dry. Add broth as needed.
4. After 30 minutes, remove lid. Add enough broth to make sauce consistency.
5. Remove herb sprigs. You can leave garlic in or take it out.
6. At this point you can use sauce or you can puree in a processor.

1. The type and quality of your tomatoes will change the flavor of your sauce. Experiment with different ones until you find your favorite.
2. You can substitute one shallot for onion if you wish. You can also add sweet peppers at this stage.
3. Once you crush your garlic, leave it intact.
4. You can use a single herb or combination. Marjoram also works nice.
5. Taste as you go with the olive oil and adjust TT
6. Salt and add red pepper sparingly at the end. You can always add more TT at the table.

Your Notes:

Sassy BBQ Sauce

Store bought BBQ sauce tastes like, well, store bought compared to this easy sauce. Honestly, it is worth the time and makes left over chicken and pork something you want left over! I roast a whole chicken and reserve the breast meat for this recipe. We serve it with Cole Slaw for a perfect balance of tang and creaminess. It is great with ground tempeh for a vegetarian dish as well. Try it on a burger with cheddar cheese – yummy!

Sassy BBQ Sauce

Ingredients

Pat	Butter (to CG pan)
2	Medium Onions minced
½ cup	Dark Rum or Bourbon
2/3 cup	Ketchup
2 Tbsp	Prepared Mustard
1/3 cup	Apple Juice
¼ cup	Maple Syrup
¼ cup	Molasses
2 Tbsp	Worcestershire Sauce
1 tsp	Garlic powder
2 Tbsp	Butter (stirred in at end)

1. You can eliminate the rum however; all the alcohol does burn off and leaves a nice flavor.
2. The mustard adds just the right amount of tang for my tastes. You can add vinegar in addition to or instead of mustard for more tang if you want,
3. You can sub orange juice for apple juice.
4. Worcestershire Sauce adds nice flavor but can be omitted.
5. You can skip the butter at the end but I find it rounds out the flavor.

Your Notes:

Directions

1. CG a 8 inch skillet and heat over medium heat. Add onions and water cook down until soft – about 5 minutes.
2. Add Rum or Bourbon and let cook down until onions are just moist.
3. Add the rest of the ingredients through garlic powder.
4. Reduce heat and simmer until sauce thickens – about 20 minutes. Remember; if you are using this to make pulled pork, chicken or tempeh, it will continue to cooks so don't let it get too thick. You can always add or broth to thin if needed.
5. Once the sauce it ready, add butter and stir into sauce before removing from heat.

Master Creamy Salad Sauce (MCSS)

The name is so long and awkward for such a simple sauce. I just did not know what to call it so...it is what it is. I adjust the ratios for this based on what I am using it for however I use this basic recipe for anything that normally calls for mayonnaise. I use store bought organic products because I have not mastered a good homemade mayo or yogurt. I know this would be that much better tasting if you do so if you are so inclined...go for it!

Master Creamy Salad Sauce

Ingredients

1 part	Organic Mayo
2 parts	Organic Whole Plain Yogurt
1 tsp per cup sauce TT	Garlic Powder
TT	Everyday Seasoning (see Master Spice blend for ingredients)

Directions

This sauce is so simple and yet so good. You will be surprised how far a little will go so GSTG for sure. The mayo brings a rich creaminess to the sauce and the yogurt offers freshness and tang. The yogurt also reduces the fat content, adds some Probiotics and helps the sauce spread over your ingredients, allowing you to use less.

1. Put the ingredients into a bowl and stir together. You can premix this sauce and store in the refrigerator for up to 2 weeks.

Add ins: Any dried herbs (dill is great), dried or prepared mustard, Sriracha sauce for a kick.

For simple and delicious creamy salads try:

- Potato
- Mock Potato made with Cauliflower
- Pasta
- Cabbage
- Broccoli
- Tuna/Salmon
- Tempeh

1. The next edition of this book will have a homemade mayo recipe. The reality is, however, I don t make it now so this is what I use.
2. You can substitute 1 part pureed avocado for the mayo for an even healthier version – just make sure you add salt TT.
3. You can sub dairy free yogurt but it must be unsweetened.
4. Please add your own spices. Be creative and adjust based on what base you are adding the sauce.

Your Notes:

YOUR
DELICIOUS
DISH
HERE!

_____

Ingredients

Directions

YOUR
DELICIOUS
DISH
HERE!

_____

Ingredients

Directions

YOUR
DELICIOUS
DISH
HERE!

Ingredients

Directions

SALADS

*Vegetables are loaded with nutrition and taste amazing!
The possibilities are endless. Tossed salads become a
meal by adding nuts, seeds or some sliced meats.
Add a good dressing and dinner is served!
Kids like to pick up their veggies and just crunch away.
Offer them a dip and they will devour a rainbow of
veggies in a single sitting. Put a variety of salads out for
a single meal, something creamy, something crunchy and
something leafy...leftovers equal lunch if you are lucky
enough to have any!*

Best Broccoli Salad

I take this to every potluck and if I don't, I hear about it. This salad gets even the "I hate vegetables" people to eat broccoli. I make both a vegan and I meat eaters' version and honestly I don't know which one I like better. The one below is vegan however I give you the recipe for both.

Best Broccoli Salad

Ingredients

4 cups	Broccoli florets and hearts of stem
1 small	Red onion diced
½ cup	Toasted Sunflower Seeds
1/3 cup	Raisins
¾ - 1 cup	MCSS
1 scant tsp TT	Smoked Paprika

Directions

1. Place all the dry ingredients into a bowl and mix.
2. In a small bowl, mix the smoked paprika and the MCSS together.
3. Add the MCSS to the dry ingredient until all the pieces are coated. Remember to GSTG the MCSS.
4. Let the salad sit for at least 15 minutes and taste. It takes a bit for the smoked paprika's' flavor to blossom. Season as needed.

Variations:

- Replace toasted seeds with 3 slices crumbled crispy bacon. Omit smoked paprika.
- Shredded Sharp Cheddar Cheese is a wonderful addition to both versions.
- You can omit the raisins and add carrots for a more subtle sweetness.

1. You can buy a bag of organic florets in most stores these days but if you buy the broccoli stalks it is a waste to just use the florets. All you need to do is remove the outer "skin" from the stalk with a knife to reveal the soft and tasty "heart". Simply chop and add to the salad.
2. Toasting the seeds enhances the flavor and texture. Just place the seeds on a cookie sheet and place in a 400 degree oven for 15 minutes, checking every 5 minutes to make sure they do not burn.
3. Try subbing pumpkin seeds and other dried fruits
4. Smoked paprika adds depth and replaces the smoked flavor of the bacon

Your Notes:

Purple Cole Slaw

Cole Slaw is a picnic staple and makes BBQ anything taste better. This version is made with antioxidant rich purple cabbage and Asian Vinaigrette. Great paired with steak or chicken with Thai Sauce. The one in the Salad's title page is made with Master Creamy Salad Sauce. It is creamy, crunchy and oh so good. Both variations you will want to keep cabbage in your vegetable keeper all year round.

Purple Cole Slaw

Ingredients

4 cups	Purple Cabbage shredded
1 small	Onion sliced thin
½ cup	Shredded Carrots
¼ cup	Cilantro
½ - 1 cup TT	Asian Vinaigrette

1. You can use white cabbage Chinese cabbage or Napa cabbage or any combination
2. Slicing the onion thin helps integrate the flavor and not make if overwhelming. Scallions can be substituted.

Your Notes:

Directions

1. Place all the dry ingredients in a medium bowl
2. Add vinaigrette until coated. GSTG

Variation:

For a creamy slaw, omit the cilantro and substitute MCSS for the vinaigrette.

Add ons: Sliced sweet peppers, cucumbers and radishes work well in both versions.

Fresh Mozzarella Salad

Caprese salad is wonderful Italian fare made with fresh mozzarella, sliced tomato and basil drizzled with olive oil and balsamic vinegar. Here I use Ciliegine which are .33 oz bite size balls mixed with fresh vegetables in balsamic vinaigrette, eliminating the need for a knife and making each bite full of flavor.

Fresh Mozzarella Salad

Ingredients

8 oz container	Ciliegine Fresh Mozzarella halved
1 large	English cucumbers quartered & sliced
1	Sweet red pepper large diced
20	Grape tomatoes halved
½	Red onion diced
TT	Fresh Basil
½ cup TT	Balsamic Vinaigrette (see directions)

1. You can use any size cheese and cut it into bite size pieces. The goal is to stretch the cheese with more veggies.
2. English cucumbers or hot house cucumbers are grown hydroponically, yielding edible skin & seeds.
3. Substitute any color pepper.
4. Scallions work too.
5. You can drizzle extra virgin olive oil and balsamic vinegar and season with salt and pepper in place of vinaigrette

Your Notes:

Directions

1. In a medium size bowl place all dry ingredients.
2. Add vinaigrette GSTG

Balsamic Vinaigrette

- ¼ cup extra virgin olive oil
- 2 Tbsp balsamic vinegar
- 1 tsp MSB or
    - ½ tsp garlic power
    - ¼ tsp salt
    - ¼ tsp black pepper

Any Way Chopped Salad

This is my answer to pasta salad since I don't eat pasta anymore. It is hearty, flavorful, filling and way more nutritious. You can add any veggies you like and any sauce you like and any cheese you like or skip the cheese; hence the name. I do add pasta to this for guest and parties. Here is my take on it, now I leave it to you!

Any Way Chopped Salad

Ingredients

½ head	Red Cabbage chopped
1 large	English Cucumber chopped
1	Sweet Pepper chopped
20	Grape Tomatoes cut in half
1	Carrots chopped
½	Red Onion chopped
½ cup TT	Balsamic Vinaigrette
¼ cup	Crumbled Bleu Cheese

Directions

1. In a medium size bowl place all dry ingredients.
2. Add vinaigrette GSTG

Balsamic Vinaigrette

- ¼ cup extra virgin olive oil
- 2 Tbsp balsamic vinegar
- 1 tsp MSB or
  - ½ tsp garlic power
  - ¼ tsp salt
  - ¼ tsp black pepper

1. These veggies work well together because they provide wonderful color, lots of crunch and are full of nutrition.
2. You can use any assortment of veggies that have on hand.
3. Use any cheese you like. Try Feta and add olives and oregano for a Greek twist. Aged Provolone is also delicious
4. Change the dressing and you have a whole different salad.
5. You can add beans, corn pasta

Your Notes:

YOUR
DELICIOUS
DISH
HERE!

_____

Ingredients

Directions

YOUR
DELICIOUS
DISH
HERE!

Ingredients

Directions

YOUR
DELICIOUS
DISH
HERE!

_____

Ingredients

Directions

PROTEIN

I am a fan of quality protein.
My experience and personal research points to the
human body's need for protein.
We can survive on lower quantities; however, I believe we
thrive when protein is a part of our daily intake.
I also believe that quality matters.
Whether you choose to acquire your protein from animals
or plants, know your source and focus on the least
processed forms as possible.

Always Pleasey Fried Eggs

My family likes their fried eggs with a runny yolk but the white completely cooked. I believe most restaurants refer to this as "over easy". After many, many, many attempts, I mastered the over but not the easy. Broken yolks were common until...I tried the water technique on eggs. With a little practice it produces the perfect marriage of sunny side up with the guarantee of the no runny white, over easy; hence the name Always Pleasey Eggs.

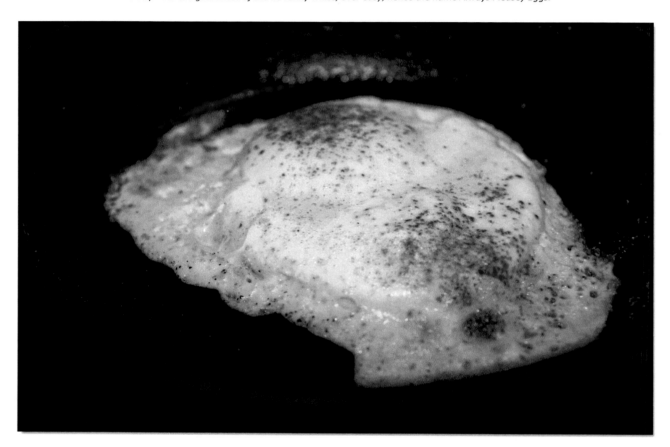

Always Pleasey Eggs

Ingredients

2 +	Eggs
CG pat	Butter
TT	MSB or other seasoning
1 Tbsp +	Water

Directions

1. CG your skillet. I suggest you use your smaller on for 1-2 eggs. You want the eggs to fill the skillet so adjust the size based on number of eggs.
2. Heat over med/hi heat until butter is shiny.
3. Crack your eggs being careful not to break the yolk.
4. Season if desired.
5. Turn heat down to medium and cover.
6. After approximately 1 minute lift cover. The egg should no longer be transparent.
7. Lift a little of the white and pour in 1 Tbsp water for 2 eggs. Steam should rise. Close the lid.
8. Let cook for another 2-3 minutes. Check to see for doneness.

The steam will seal the egg without overcooking the yolk. Once the white on top is cooked you can remove from heat. Leave in pan covered for a harder yolk or plate immediately for a runny yolk.

1. I use Organic Omega 3 eggs. If you have a source of farm fresh eggs – you are fortunate!
2. You can use a large skillet and cook several eggs at once with this method
3. Seasoning during the cooking process can take a plain old egg to the next level. If cooking for a crowd it may not work but it is worth experimenting for you and your family.

Your Notes:

Scrambled Eggs

Scrambled eggs can become a veggie lover's best friend. Sautee some left over veggies, pour scrambled eggs over them right in the pan and you have a hearty, healthy breakfast in a matter of minutes. Of course you can keep it simple and put the veggies on the side. Scrambled eggs are also perfect for feeding a crowd as they are easy to keep warm without losing texture.

Scrambled Eggs

Ingredients

6	Eggs
2 Tbsp	Water
TT	Seasonings
CG pat	Butter

Directions

1. CG your skillet. 8 inch skillet works well with 6 eggs.
2. Crack eggs into medium bowl. Add liquid of choice. Season if desired.
3. Whisk together until a lemony yellow color is achieved.
4. Heat skillet over med/hi heat.
5. Once pan is hot and butter is shiny, pour in eggs.
6. Turn heat down to medium.
7. Using a wood spatula, slowly scrape cooked egg from the bottom of the pan allowing the raw egg to flow into its place.
8. Continue until egg is almost completely cooked.
9. Turn off heat.
10. Continue scraping motion until egg is cooked through and plate immediately as to not overcook and dry out the eggs.

If using veggies, heat them first and the pour eggs over the heated veggies and proceed. If you would like to add cheese, do so once you turn off the heat and scramble into egg.

1. I find 6 eggs scrambled will feed 4 people – feel free to adjust.
2. You can sub milk, yogurt, sour cream, coconut milk for water. The purpose of the added liquid is to bring the yolks and whites together and improved the texture. My personal favorite is yogurt.
3. As with the fried eggs, I like to season the eggs and then cook them.

Your Notes:

Omelets

Looking for a special weekend breakfast? How does a fluffy omelet filled with your heart's desire sound? Veggies, meat, cheese, potatoes topped with salsa or pesto? We make Sunday Pizza Egg with mushrooms, cheese and topped with Tomato Sauce. YUM! You can fold them over or just leave them flat. Whatever you choose, make sure you take your time to cook the egg and you will be rewarded with a delicious and nutritious meal.

Omelets

Ingredients

4	Eggs
2 Tbsp	Water
CG pat	Butter
TT	Seasoning
TT	Filling
TT	Toppings
2Tbsp +	Water for WC

Directions

1. CG your skillet.
2. Crack eggs into a medium bowl. Add liquid of choice and season if desired.
3. Whisk together until a lemony yellow color is achieved.
4. Heat skillet over med/hi heat.
5. Once pan is hot and butter is shiny, pour in eggs.
6. Turn heat down to medium and cover.
7. After approximately 1 minute lift cover. The egg should no longer be transparent.
8. Lift an edge and pour in 1 Tbsp of water. Steam should rise. Close the lid.
9. After about 2 more minutes, check egg. Once only the top of the egg is liquid, add toppings. Cover
10. After 1 minute check the egg. If it is set or almost set, turn off heat. If leaving open face you can add cheese at this point and cover. If folding fold now and add cheese, cover.
11. Remove egg from pan and serve.

1. If you want to make individual omelets, 2 eggs in the 5 inch skillet works best with an unfolded omelet. If you prefer to make a large omelet that you can share, 4 eggs in the 8 inch skillet works great. This allows the egg to spread and fold easily.
2. As with scrambled eggs, you can substitute the water with another liquid of your choice.
3. The fillings and toppings are up to you. Just remember, if you want to fold it over, you should not over fill.

Your Notes:

Tofu

Tofu has been a staple in Asian cuisine for centuries. Each town had its own producer and it was used as a compliment to a meal, not as an entrée. I share this because Tofu is a processed food and soybeans are often genetically modified. Organic soy is does contain GMO's under current organic standards. When preparing tofu, keep in mind it absorbs whatever flavors you put with it and tastes best when you marinate it for at least 1 hour.

Tofu

Directions

Tofu comes in 4 basic textures; soft, firm, extra firm and silken. Silken usually comes in shelf stable packaging and is best used as a base for creamy dips and desserts. The other 3, soft, firm and extra firm tofu come packed in water and are found in the refrigerated section. They can be used interchangeably to fry, grill, crumble and roast. I will share with how I prepare tofu and if you decide to incorporate tofu into your eating plan, there are tons of resources and recipes out there.

I like a "meaty" texture. There are a couple of ways to achieve this. Both methods require you to remove the tofu from the water.

- One is to press the water out off the tofu. You simply slice the tofu to the desired thickness called for in your recipe. You then place the tofu on paper towels, put a few more on top and put something on top of it and literally press the water out. This takes a few hours.
- Or...you can take the tofu out of the water and put into a freezer safe container and pop in the freezer upon purchase. When you want to use it, defrost overnight and slice. Freezing naturally pulls the moisture out.

Once you have removed some of the water you now need to marinate it. The tofu pictured was marinated in the chimichurra sauce. Most tofu marinades are based in soy sauce however you can be creative.

Once the tofu has been marinated for at least an hour, you can bake it, grill it, or crumble it for tacos or sloppy joes.

Tempting Tempeh

Of all the soy products, tempeh is by far my favorite both for nutrition and flavor. Tempeh uses whole cooked soybeans and is then fermented using tempeh starter. This fermentation binds the soybeans resulting in a soybean cake called tempeh. Unlike tofu, which is actually made from soy milk, tempeh is a whole food. Its texture is meaty and satisfying. Below is tempeh salad which requires steaming. You can also grill and pan fry tempeh with delicious results.

Tempting Tempeh

Ingredients

One 16oz	Tempeh cake
½ cup TT	MCSS or mayo
2	Scallions diced
TT	Seasonings

Directions

Yes, this is a simple recipe and you can easily substitute canned tuna or salmon for the tempeh. Just because it's easy does not mean it is not delicious and nutritious.

1. Steam tempeh in a steam basket for about 10 minutes. (you can use the steam tower method and make your base for dinner at the same time!)
2. Once the tempeh is warmed through and softened, remove from heat.
3. Let it cool down and crumble into a medium sized bowl. Add MCSS or mayo, seasoning and veggies.
4. Stir to combine.
5. Refrigerate for 20 minutes or more to let flavors develop.

Add ins: sweet peppers, relish, roasted red peppers, olives, celery, radish, Jicama, shredded carrots. For seasoning try some cayenne, dill or oregano. Fresh herbs are also delicious.

1. There are several varieties of tempeh on the market. Try them and pick your favorite.
2. Any creamy dressing will work here. Homemade ranch, yogurt, plain mayo….
3. Any onion will do…or you can omit.
4. The MCSS is already seasoned, however if you are using mayonnaise or other creamy dressing, you may want to season

Your Notes:

Nuts and Seeds

Healthy fats, protein and fiber make these little guys energy powerhouses. Raw food enthusiasts create amazing things out of these simple treasures. However you don't need to get fancy to reap the benefits. Toss them in a salad, grind them into your burgers or just pop a few into your mouth for a satisfying snack. Don't forget the nut butters! Spread some almond butter on an apple and you have a quick and healthy breakfast on the go.

Nuts and Seeds

Directions

The nutrition and digestibility of most nuts and seeds is enhanced by soaking. While the soaking times vary by variety, if you soak them overnight in the refrigerator, you have most of your bases covered.

1. Use a glass container large enough to fit your nuts or seeds plus 3 inches on the top.
2. Pour enough fresh cold water over the nuts or seeds to cover plus 2 inches.
3. Cover and refrigerate overnight.
4. In the morning, drain all the water and rinse. You can now use them, store them in a clean container and refrigerate for up to 4 days or spread them in a single layer on a cookie sheet an place in the oven at the lowest setting (150 degrees) and dry for about 4 hours or until dry. Drying will prolong their freshness.

*Walnuts do not need to be soaked but you can.

**Flax seeds benefit from toasting at 200 degrees for 30 minutes – no need to soak first.

The Whole Chicken

I get at least 2 if not 3 meals out of every whole chicken I roast. I always make chicken broth and if I am lucky, I have enough meat to make my BBQ pulled chicken. Roasted whole chicken is a deceivingly easy yet elegant meal. While I keep the seasoning simple using my master spice blend, you can get crazy. Garlic under the skin, Indian Tandoori spices, blackening spices all work great. The veggies melt in your mouth and the flavors come together beautifully. Use low carb veggies and starchy veggies to make this a one pot meal made in a pan.

The Whole Chicken Dinner

Ingredients

2.5 – 3 lb	Whole chicken
2 Tbsp +	MSB or other dry seasonings
2 medium	Onions quartered
3 medium	Red Potatoes quartered
¼ head	Red Cabbage cut in large chunks
1 cup +	Water

Directions

Preheat oven to 400 degrees and get a roasting pan out.

1. Remove packaging from chicken and remove giblets. Rinse chicken, including cavity and pat dry with paper towels.
2. Place chicken breast side up and rub half with half your seasonings.
3. Flip you chicken so breast side is down and rub back with remaining seasonings. Toss any extra into the cavity. (Roast the chicken breast side down. By seasoning in the roasting pan, any loose spices will flavor your veggies and broth)
4. Center the chicken in the pan and place your veggies around it. I put the onions close to the chicken for extra flavor.
5. Pour water into bottom of the pan so that the veggies are almost covered but not swimming.
6. Place chicken in oven uncovered and roast for 30 minutes.
7. Turn oven down to 350 and continue to roast for 60 minutes – checking occasionally to make sure there is enough liquid in the pan and the top of the chicken is not burning. Add liquid if needed. If top is getting burnt, place a parchment lined piece of foil over the top. No need to secure it – simply crease it in the center and make a tent.
8. Chicken is done when the internal temp is 170 degrees and the juices run clear when pierced with a knife.

1. This is a standard weight for whole chicken in the supermarket. You will just need to adjust your cooking time for more or less weight.
2. Since I use the bones to make broth, I insist on using an organic chicken.
3. You can use any root or hearty vegetables for this meal.
   a. Onion
   b. Carrots
   c. sweet potato (my fav)
   d. turnips
   e. cauliflower
   f. sweet peppers
   g. fennel
   h. celery

Your Notes:

Golden Drumsticks

Drumsticks or chicken legs are an economical way to feed a large group and kids love chomping on this finger friendly food. The golden color comes from turmeric. Turmeric is noted for its many health benefits and it makes this meal glow. Marinating drumsticks improves both the flavor and texture. They roast up quickly and taste great cold making them a good choice for picnic fare.

Golden Drumsticks

Ingredients

10	Drumsticks
2 cups	Plain whole milk yogurt
2 Tbsp	Turmeric
3	Garlic cloves minced
2 tsp	Salt
1 tsp	Cumin

Directions

The flavors take time to blend. I suggest allowing the chicken to sit in the marinade for at least 6 hours or overnight. If you make it in the morning for dinner that night, you are good to go.

1. Place chicken into an oven safe dish in a single layer not squished.
2. In a medium bowl, combine yogurt (coconut milk) spices and herbs.
3. Pour the sauce over the chicken and completely cover. Shake it around to make sure sauce goes under and all around.
4. Cover and put in fridge for at least 6 hours.

To cook: Preheat oven to 350 degrees.

1. Uncover chicken and carefully pour marinade into the sink leaving enough to coat the bottom of the dish.
2. Cover chicken with parchment lined foil.
3. Place in oven and cook for 45 minutes.
4. Remove cover and cook for an additional 15 minutes.
5. Chicken is done when it reached 165 degrees and juices run clear when pierced with a knife.

1. If you can find organic drumsticks, they are still a great deal and worth it.
2. Coconut milk is wonderful as well. Try it for a dairy free version or just for an exotic twist.
3. Turmeric makes the color pop in this dish, however you can use any spice blend you want.
4. Garlic really adds to the flavor. If you omit, make sure you add some fragrant herbs.

Your Notes:

Killer Thighs

Chicken Thighs offer the versatility of chicken breast without the expense. They cook up moist and flavorful every time. and freeze well so buying in bulk is another way to save. They taste great pan fried with just some simple seasoning or pour tomato sauce over the cooked chicken while still in the pan; top it with cheese and cover on for 5 minutes for a quick chicken parm. Steam tower pasta and zucchini ribbons, slice a cucumber and you have dinner in less than 30 minutes.

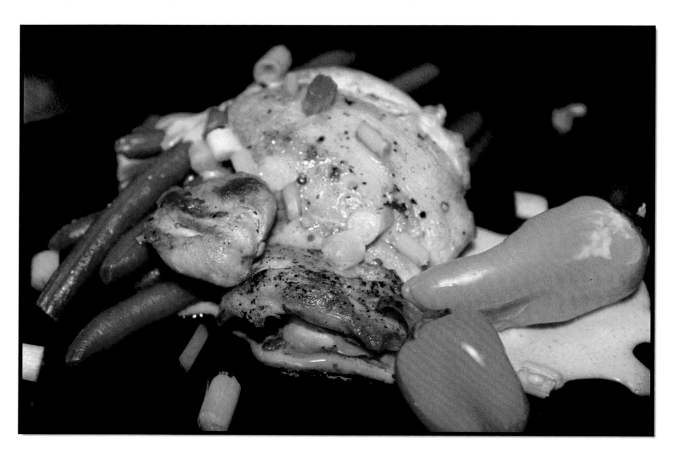

Killer Thighs

Ingredients

6-8	Chicken Thighs
TT	MSB or other Seasoning
CG pat	Butter

Directions

It's so simple. This chicken tastes great and works for those who like to keep to the basics. Add sauce and you capture the sophisticated palate as well. The picture on the facing page features the Thai Peanut sauce served over sautéed beans. Add some rice and there is a meal everyone can enjoy.

1. CG a skillet and heat on med/hi heat until butter is shiny.
2. Place thigh in a single layer in the hot pan.
3. Season and cover.
4. After about 5 minutes, uncover, flip the chicken and season the other side.
5. Cover pan again.
6. Chicken is done when juices run clear when pierce with a knife.

1. The key to versatility is in the seasoning and the sauces. Thighs provide a moist and delicious base for whatever you fancy.
   a. Taco blend, some sautéed onions and peppers and its fajitas.
   b. Curry powder, pour in some coconut milk and you have an Indian dish to go over rice and cauliflower.
   c. Add a little soy, ginger and sesame oil in the pan after the chicken is cooked and serve with sautéed green beans and angel hair pasta. Who needs take out.

Your Notes:

Simply Steak

Outside of cuts like london broil which really benefits from marinating, I use the same basic cooking approach for most steaks, my favorite is skirt steak. A good steak speaks for itself and the less I do the better it tastes. I find following the steps and not rushing the process, produces the best results. Toss up a colorful salad with a flavorful dressing and dinner is served.

Simply Steak

Ingredients

Your choice of	Steak
TT	Salt
TT	Pepper
CG pat	Butter
1	Clove Garlic raw not crushed

1. Finding the best cut of a steak will vary based on the tastes of the diner.
2. While some people prefer their steak cooked medium well to well, I suggest you try medium rare to medium temperature. It makes for a more flavorful and healthful piece of meat.

Your Notes:

Directions

1. 30 minutes prior to cooking, take steak out of refrigerator. Plate and season with salt on both sides. Let steak come to room temperature, about 20 minutes.
2. At 20 minutes, prepare your pan. Take garlic and rub the pan as if you were cold greasing. Then CG your pan with butter.
3. Heat over medium high heat until butter is shiny.
4. Place steak in skillet. If using pepper, season now.
5. Cooking time will depend on thickness of steak and desired temperature. The majority of the cooking time should occur PRIOR to flipping the steak. The best way to test is to push the steak with your finger (being careful not to get burned). If it squishes down a lot, it is rare, a little is medium and barely is well. You can also look on the side of the steak and see how far down the red goes. The more red the less cooked.
6. Once you feel the steak is close to done, flip it and cook for about another 1-2 minutes. Do the finger test again. Take your steak off when it is not quite done since it will continue to cook off the heat.
7. Place the steak on a warm plate and cover to rest for 10 minutes before serving.

MoKa Joe Pork Tenderloin

Pork Tenderloin is a go to favorite when time is short. Without a lot of prep or hands on cooking, you will be surprised how impressive this meat turns out. I use various rubs depending on what side dishes I can throw together. Pork pairs nicely with something a little sweet and is often served with a chutney, cooked fruit or rubbed with a little sugar. I also love using an Asian rub and serving it with wasabi mashed potatoes/cauliflower

MoKa Joe Pork Tenderloin

Ingredients

Two, 1 – 1.5 lb	Pork tenderloins
2 Tbsp	Coffee grounds (extra fine grind)
1 Tbsp	Unsweetened cocoa
2 tsp	Cinnamon
1 tsp	Garlic powder
2 tsp TT	Salt
2 Tbsp	Sugar (optional)

Directions

Many recipes suggest you sear the tenderloin before roasting. I only sear if I am not using a rub. To sear: CG your skillet. When butter is shiny, put in pork and cook on med/hi. Turn occasionally until all sides are browned. This step reduces the cooking time to about 15 minutes but is more hands on. Searing is not necessary with a rub.

1. Tender loins often have a silver skin that can be tough when cooked. To remove use a small sharp knife and slide the blade under and out.
2. Preheat the oven to 425.
3. Prepare the rub and evenly coat both tenderloins well.
4. Place into oven safe pan and put in oven.
5. Cook uncovered for about 25 minutes or until internal temp reaches 145 degrees. This temp will avoid drying out the tenderloin. It should be slightly pink in the middle.
6. Remove from oven and cover. Let rest 10 minutes before serving.

1. Look at the ingredients of the tenderloin and aim for one that has not been injected with a bunch of flavor enhances – pork and maybe salt should be it.
2. You can espresso coffee ground.. If using drip ground coffee, use a spice blender or mortar and pestle to get a finer grind.
3. Hot cocoa mix will not work here.
4. I serve this with the Harvest Chutney which is sweet so I omit the sugar. If you don't plan on having a sweet component at the meal, you can use the sugar for better flavor balance.
5. Asian Rub: first coat tenderloin with a mixture of 1 Tbsp soy sauce and 1 Tbsp toasted sesame oil
   a. 3 Tbsp sesame seeds
   b. 2 Tbsp brown sugar
   c. 1 Tbsp ground ginger
   d. 1 tsp garlic powder
   e. 1 tsp wasabi powder

Your Notes:

A Burger by Many Other Names

One day a burger, the next day meatballs and then magically meatloaf ... Ground meat, some spices and viola something delicious awaits. I use the same basic recipe and by changing up the meat, spices and shape you'd never know. Mix up the presentation and even more creative meals can come from this humble recipe.

A Burger by Many Other Names

Ingredients

1 lb	Ground meat
1	Egg
¼ cup	Ground flax seeds
1 Tbsp TT	MSB or other spices

Directions

1. In a medium size bowl, combine egg, flax and spices
2. Whisk together until egg is completely integrated.
3. Add meat. Then using your hands, thoroughly mix everything together creating a uniform mixture.
4. Now you can form them into meat balls, hamburgers, meatloaf, meat dogs (hamburgers shaped like a hot dog).

Meats to try: Turkey, Beef, Buffalo, Lamb, Bison, Venison, Chicken

Spices and Shapes:

- Turkey meat dogs made with taco seasoning served in a taco shell (less mess and lots of fun)
- Lamb burgers with rosemary, garlic and salt served in a pita or lettuce leaf drizzled with cucumber yogurt sauce
- Beef meatballs made with Italian seasoning served on top of spaghetti, over zucchini ribbons or in a roll for meatball sandwiches
- Chicken with nutmeg, coriander, dry mustard and oregano for a healthy bratwurst.

Different meats will yield unique flavors. Try combining meats as well. I often combine 1 lb turkey with 1 lb grass fed beef.

1. This recipe can easily be double, tripled or beyond.
2. Use 1 egg for up to 3 pounds meat – 2 eggs for 4-6 pounds.
3. Add an additional Tbsp of flax for each additional pound of meat. The flax takes the place of bread crumbs and helps retain moister and adds fiber.
4. If you multiply the recipe you can make various shapes and freeze.

Your Notes:

YOUR
DELICIOUS
DISH
HERE!

_____

Ingredients

Directions

YOUR
DELICIOUS
DISH
HERE!

_____

Ingredients

Directions

YOUR
DELICIOUS
DISH
HERE!

Ingredients

Directions

Your Notes:

129

YOUR
DELICIOUS
DISH
HERE!

_____

Ingredients

Directions

131

BASES

Pasta without sauce, bread without butter,
oats without maple, you just don't see it. In general,
grains, breads and starches act as a base for other
flavors. They also provide various nutrients,
carbohydrates and fiber.
For some people these carbohydrates are part of a sound
eating style and for others they are not.
Many people are discovering they function better by
limiting starchy carbohydrates and focusing on
non-starchy vegetables instead. This section briefly
covers the basic methods for preparing both starchy and
non starchy bases since really...
"It's all in the sauce"
.

Starches

I prepare rice, pasta, grains and potatoes using basically the same method. As for beans, soaking and boiling beans is simple and like making home my own mayo, I should do it, however I don't. We do not consume a lot of beans so on the occasions that we do, I buy organic canned beans. I also make risotto and simply follow the directions on the package. I encourage you explore some of the ancient grains and decide if they fit into your approach.

Starches

Directions

PASTA: There is no magic here. I simply follow the directions on the package. The key to good pasta is to not overcook and create mush. This is especially true when using gluten free pasta.

1. Fill a sauce pan ¾ of the way full of cold water. Leave pot uncovered.
2. Bring water to a rolling boil.
3. Add desired amount of pasta.
4. Return to boil and continue to cook.
5. Check for doneness after recommended time (usually 8-10 minutes)
6. If not done, check every 1-2 minutes
7. Drain in colander and rinse with fresh water.

If not saucing the pasta right away, rinse with cold water, return to pan and coat with olive oil to prevent sticking.

RICE: Years ago my mom read that you could cook rice like pasta to reduce stickiness. I tried it and ever since that is how I cook rice. I also like this method because it eliminates the issues around the water to rice ratio and avoids the rice burnt on the bottom syndrome I often encountered. NOTE: for this method to work, you must use at least 3 parts water to 1 part rice – although if you have enough room in your pot, I suggest a 4:1 ratio.

1. Place rice in a bowl and fill with water. Let sit for 5-10 minutes. Drain water and rinse rice with fresh water 1 -2 times until rinse water is not longer cloudy.
2. Fill a sauce pan ¾ of the way full of cold water. Leave pot uncovered.
3. Bring water to a rolling boil.
4. Add desired amount of rice.
5. Return to boil and continue to cook rice as you would pasta.
6. Once rice is al dente (still a little hard) you will proceed depending on how you want to use the rice
   a. If using plain, continue to cook to desired doneness and drain in a fine colander.
   b. If you would like to flavor your rice using broth or seasonings drain rice while still al dente. Return to pot and stove. Add broth or seasoned water, starting with ½ cup and stirring until absorbed. Continue adding liquid until desired doneness.

POTATOES: This method is for boiled potatoes that can be used for mashed potatoes, potato salad, home fries etc. I leave the skins on when boiling. If I want to remove them, I can peel the skin off using my fingers easily after they are done, although I usually just leave them on for more flavor, texture and nutrition. It's up to you.

1. Wash potatoes and leave skin intact.
2. Cut potatoes into equal pieces approximately 1 – 1 ½ inches each.
3. Fill sauce pan ¾ way full and bring to rolling boil.
4. Add potatoes.
5. Cook as you would pasta.
6. Potatoes are done if you can pierce them through with a fork.
7. Drain potatoes. You can mash them at this point or let them cool to make potato salad or your favorite potato dish.
8. If you want to peel off the skins, rinse potatoes with cold water and peel.

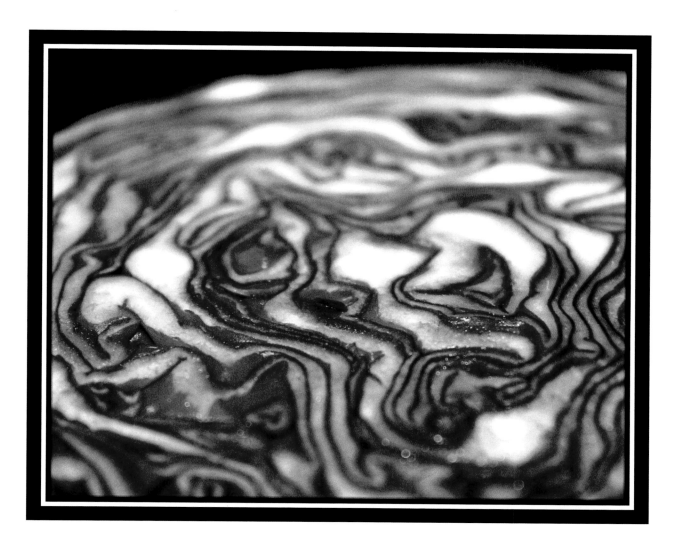

Low Carb Veggies

I love using veggies as my base for delicious sauces. I find the flavors and textures pleasant and satiating. I often wrap my "sandwich" in a lettuce or collard green leaf with a smear of pesto or drizzled with chimmi sauce. Salad serves as a bed for a burger or steak. Pork with pureed cauliflower is wonderful and chicken with sautéed green beans is a family hit. If you are not having a sauce, simply add a little olive oil or butter and salt at the end of the sauté and you will not miss the pasta!

Directions

FRESH VEGETABLES: All fresh veggies other than greens start out getting steamed. If I do not use the steam tower method I will steam them on their own. This maintains the nutrients and reduces the cooking time in the skillet.

To steam:

1. Place approximately 1 inch of water into a pan that your steam basket fits or use the ST method.
2. Put veggies into the basket. They can be cozy but overcrowding will result in them not cooking evenly.
3. Place steam basket over water and cover.
4. Allow to steam for 5-10 minutes depending on density of vegetable. You can decide how cooked you want them. I suggest once you can pierce easily with a knife, you take them off the water. The exception is cauliflower which I steam until soft like potatoes.
5. Once they are done steaming you can serve as is or sauté.

To sauté:

1. Cold grease your skillet or use the drippings from whatever meat you cooked.
2. Heat the pan over med/hi heat.
3. Place veggies in and stir them around.
4. Turn heat down to medium and cover.
5. After 3-5 minutes lift cover and stir. Veggies should start to brown but not burn. Add a little water to WC if needed.
6. Once all the water has evaporated and veggies are heated through, turn off heat.
7. Season with MSB or other seasons. Add a touch of butter or olive oil to coat for extra flavor and healthy fat.

FROZEN VEG AND GREENS: I use water cooking when preparing my greens and frozen vegetable. Because most vegetables are blanched before freezing steaming them is redundant and produces mushy results.

1. Following the sauté instructions above using the WC method to prevent the vegetables from sticking.

Your Creations

YOUR

DELICIOUS

DISH

HERE!

Ingredients

Directions

YOUR
DELICIOUS
DISH
HERE!

_____

Ingredients

Directions

145

YOUR
DELICIOUS
DISH
HERE!

_____

Ingredients

Directions

YOUR
DELICIOUS
DISH
HERE!

Ingredients

Directions

YOUR
DELICIOUS
DISH
HERE!

_____

Ingredients

Directions

Index

Made in the USA
Middletown, DE
04 March 2016